S

TRAVE   GUIDE

SCENIC TOURS

Copyright © 2023 Scenic Tours

This Sicily Travel Guide is owned and published by Scenic Tours. All content within this publication is the property of Scenic Tours and is protected under international copyright laws.

Table of Contents

DISCLAIMER

The information contained in this Sicily Travel Guide is provided as a general guide only. While every effort has been made to ensure the accuracy of the information contained herein, the author and publisher make no representations or warranties of any kind with respect to the accuracy, relevancy, or completeness of the content of this guide. The reader should exercise due caution and discretion while using this guide. The author and publisher shall not be liable for any losses or damages incurred as a result of the use of this guide.

AN ODE TO SICILIAN TOURISTS

Of Sicilian tourists, I must sing,

For they bring joy to everything.

With hearts as warm as the Mediterranean sun,

They light up the island, one by one.

From Taormina to Ustica's shores,

They come to see the sea's treasures and explore.

With laughter ringing through the air,

Their joy is something truly rare.

They come from near and far,

To bask in Sicily's shining star.

To taste the flavors of the land,

And walk upon its ancient sands.

With hearts as big as Mount Etna's flames,

They make us feel like we're all the same.

Their smiles light up the darkest night,

And make us feel like everything's all right.

So here's to you, dear Sicilian tourists,

For filling our hearts with memories that endure

May your joy and light continue to shine,

And may you always find a home here in this land divine

A GLIMPSE OF SICILY

Sicily, the biggest island in the Mediterranean Sea, is an appealing location with a range of attractions. Situated off the point of the Italian mainland, Sicily is the biggest area in Italy and is home to some of the world's most spectacular landscapes, cultural riches, and interesting history. Sicily is an island with a rich and varied history, having been colonized by the Greeks, Romans, Arabs, Normans and Bourbons all having had their effect on the island. Sicily's unique history and cultural influences have developed a distinct and diversified culture that attracts tourists from all over the world.

Sicily's spectacular environment, with its mountains, valleys, beaches, and volcanic landscapes, pulls in travelers looking to enjoy the island's natural beauty. One of the most famous tourist attractions in Sicily is Mount Etna, the biggest active volcano in Europe. The volcano's periodic eruptions make it a stunning site to see, and its lava flows and ash deposits have produced distinctive landscapes in the surrounding areas. Additional natural attractions in Sicily include the Aeolian Islands, a series of volcanic islands located off the northern coast of the island, and the Zingaro Natural Reserve, a protected section of coastline containing beautiful beaches and wildlife.

The cultural attractions of Sicily are similarly spectacular.
Sicily is home to a number of UNESCO World Heritage
Sites, including the Valley of the Temples, a collection of
ancient Greek temples, the Cathedral of Monreale, a
spectacular Norman church, and the Villa Romana del
Casale, an amazing Roman palace.

Visitors to Sicily may also explore the island's lively
cultural scene, with its numerous art galleries and
museums, or take in a performance of the island's
traditional folk music.

Sicily is also home to some of the world's greatest food. The island's Mediterranean climate and excellent soil make it a perfect spot to raise a variety of fresh vegetables, and its diverse culinary culture has been inspired by its numerous conquerors.

Sicily's cuisine is recognized for its use of fresh fish and vegetables, coupled with olive oil, garlic, tomatoes, and fresh herbs. Regional delicacies include arancini, sardines, and caponata, while the island's sweet pleasures, such cannoli and granita, are appreciated across the world.

Sicily is an island where tourists may appreciate the majesty of nature, learn its rich history, and enjoy its vibrant culture and cuisine. Whether guests are searching for a calm beach break or an excursion into the past, Sicily provides something for everyone.

Geography

Sicily is a land of contrasts and surprises, with a rich cultural and natural heritage that has fascinated visitors for centuries. Its position at the crossroads of the Mediterranean has made it a melting pot of different civilizations, each leaving their mark on the island's geography, architecture, and traditions.

One of the most striking features of Sicily is its mountains. The island is dominated by three main ranges: the Nebrodi in the north, the Madonie in the center, and the Iblei in the south. The highest peak is Mount Etna, a massive stratovolcano that is visible from almost anywhere on the island. Etna is not only a geological wonder, but also an important source of fertility for the surrounding lands, thanks to its rich volcanic soil. The mountain is a popular destination for hiking, skiing, and sightseeing, with several visitor centers and cable cars providing access to its summit.

The coastline is also an important part of Sicily's geography. The island has over 1,000 kilometers of shoreline, with a mix of sandy beaches, rocky cliffs, and hidden coves. The most popular beaches are located on the east and south coasts, where the water is clear and warm, and the scenery is breathtaking. Some of the most iconic beaches include San Vito lo Capo, a long crescent of golden sand backed by rugged mountains, and Isola Bella, a tiny islet connected to the mainland by a thin strip of sand.

The climate is influenced by its position in the Mediterranean, with hot, dry summers and mild, rainy winters. It enjoys over 300 days of sunshine per year, making it a popular destination for sun-seekers and outdoor enthusiasts. The mild temperatures and fertile soil also make Sicily a prime agricultural region, with a wide range of crops grown throughout the year. The island is famous for its citrus fruits, such as oranges, lemons, and mandarins, as well as for its olives, grapes, and almonds.

Sicily's history is as varied as its geography, with a complex mix of cultures and traditions that have shaped its identity over the centuries. The island has been inhabited since prehistoric times, and has been ruled by Greeks, Romans, Arabs, Normans, and Spaniards, among others. Each civilization has left its mark on the island's architecture, language, and customs, creating a unique blend of styles and influences. Some of the most iconic landmarks of Sicily include the Valley of the Temples in Agrigento, a UNESCO World Heritage Site that features some of the best-preserved Greek ruins outside Greece, and the Arab-Norman Palermo and the Cathedral Churches of Cefalù and Monreale, also recognized as UNESCO World Heritage sites.

The economy is based on a mix of traditional and modern industries. Agriculture and fishing are still important sources of income for many Sicilians, especially in rural areas. The island's fertile soil and favorable climate make it a prime location for growing fruits, vegetables, and cereals, as well as for producing wine and olive oil. Fishing is also a vital industry, with the island's rich waters providing a bountiful harvest of seafood, including tuna, swordfish, and octopus. Tourism is another major contributor to the local economy, with millions of visitors flocking to the island each year to enjoy its natural beauty, cultural heritage, and culinary delights.

Sicily is a region of extraordinary beauty and diversity, with a rich history and a vibrant culture that have made it a top destination for travelers from around the world. Its mountains, beaches, and historical landmarks offer endless opportunities for exploration and discovery, while its agricultural traditions and culinary heritage provide a feast for the senses

Culture

Sicily is a land of rich history and a culture that is as diverse as it is unique. It has been shaped by a multitude of different civilizations over the centuries, each leaving their own imprint on the island's language, art, cuisine, and traditions.

The earliest known inhabitants of Sicily were the Sicani, followed by the Phoenicians, who established the first trade networks on the island in the 9th century BC. This was followed by the Greeks, who established a number of colonies on the island in the 8th century BC. The Roman Empire also left its mark on Sicily, as did the Vandals, the Ostrogoths, and the Byzantines. However, it was the Arab conquest in the 9th century AD that had perhaps the most profound impact on the island's culture and language.

Today, the language spoken in Sicily is a unique blend of Italian, Sicilian, and Arabic, with influences from other languages such as Greek, Spanish, and French. This linguistic diversity is just one aspect of the island's rich cultural heritage. Sicilian cuisine is also a testament to the island's diverse cultural influences, with a blend of Mediterranean and African flavors.

The cuisine is known for its emphasis on seafood, fresh herbs, and spices, as well as its use of locally-grown fruits and vegetables. Some of the most popular dishes include pasta alla norma, caponata, and arancini.

Sicily is also renowned for its rich artistic traditions, which draw from a variety of different cultural influences.

Traditional Sicilian music is a fusion of folk and classical styles, with a heavy emphasis on the use of instruments such as the mandolin and the guitar. Modern music in Sicily is often a mix of pop and rock, with artists such as Franco Battiato and Carmen Consoli gaining international acclaim.

Art is also an integral part of Sicilian culture, with a number of museums and galleries showcasing the works of both local and international artists. Religious architecture is also a prominent feature of the island's art scene, with numerous churches, cathedrals, and other religious sites displaying a range of architectural styles from different periods in Sicily's history.

In addition to its rich cultural heritage, Sicily is also known for its stunning natural landscapes. The island is home to some of the most beautiful beaches in the Mediterranean, as well as mountainous regions and lush valleys. The region is also known for its vineyards and olive groves, which produce some of the finest wines and olive oils in the world.

Sicily is also a region of festivals and celebrations, with a range of events held throughout the year that showcase the island's rich cultural heritage. The Feast of St. Rosalia in Palermo and the Festival of San Patrizio in Catania are just a few examples of the many festivals held in the region each year.

Overall, Sicily is a region of great cultural and historical significance, with a unique blend of languages, art, cuisine, and traditions that reflect the island's rich and diverse heritage. Whether you are drawn to the island for its stunning natural landscapes, its vibrant cultural scene, or its delicious cuisine, Sicily is sure to leave a lasting impression on anyone who visits.

What to Expect When Visiting Sicily

Sicilians are known for their warm hospitality and friendly nature, and you can expect to be welcomed with open arms wherever you go. Family is at the heart of Sicilian culture, and you may be invited to share a meal or a glass of wine with locals during your travels. Sicilians are also passionate about their traditions and love to share them with visitors, so don't be afraid to ask questions and immerse yourself in the local culture.

Another notable aspect of Sicilian culture is its love for festivals and celebrations. You can expect to encounter a lively atmosphere during your trip, especially during the summer months when most of the festivals are held. Some of the most popular festivals in Sicily include the Feast of St. Rosalia in Palermo, the Palio di Provenzano in Enna, and the Festival of San Patrizio in Catania. These festivals are an opportunity to immerse yourself in Sicilian culture and traditions, with parades, fireworks, music, and plenty of food and drinks.

Sicilian cuisine is one of the highlights of any trip to Sicily. The island's cuisine is a blend of Mediterranean and North African flavors, with fresh seafood, pasta, and local vegetables taking center stage.

Some of the most popular dishes include pasta alla norma, which is made with eggplant, tomato sauce, and ricotta cheese, arancini, which are stuffed rice balls, and caponata, which is a sweet and sour eggplant relish.

Be sure to also try the local wine, such as Nero d'Avola or Grillo, and the famous Sicilian desserts, such as cannoli, cassata, and granita.

If you are planning to travel to Sicily, you can expect a truly unique and diverse experience. As the largest island in the Mediterranean Sea, Sicily boasts a rich history, vibrant culture, stunning landscapes, delicious cuisine, and warm hospitality.

PLANNING YOUR TRIP

When to Visit

Weather

Sicily has a Mediterranean climate, which means that it enjoys hot, dry summers and mild, wet winters. Summers (June to August) are generally hot and dry, with temperatures reaching an average of 30°C (86°F). The nights can be cooler, so it's a good idea to bring a light jacket or sweater.

Winters (December to February) are mild and wet, with temperatures ranging from 8°C (46°F) to 16°C (60°F). It can also be quite windy, so it's best to bring a windbreaker or a coat.

Holidays and Events

Sicily is home to a wide range of festivals and events throughout the year. These events offer a great opportunity to experience Sicilian culture, cuisine, and traditions. One of the most famous events is Carnevale, which takes place in February. It's a vibrant and colorful celebration with parades, costumes, and street parties. Another popular event is the Palermo Film Festival, which takes place in July and August, and features screenings of the latest films from around the world.

Other festivals and events include Easter celebrations, which are marked by processions and music; Festa di San Giovanni, a religious festival celebrating St. John the Baptist; Festa di San Giuseppe, a celebration of traditional Italian food, music, and dancing; Festa della Madonna della Lettera, which is celebrated with traditional music, processions, and fireworks; the International Puppet Festival, which is held in September and features puppet shows and performances; Festa di Santa Rosalia, which is celebrated with parades and processions; and Festa di San Martino, which is a celebration of traditional foods and music.

• Carnevale (February): Celebrate with a parade and plenty of street parties.

- Easter (March/April): Celebrate with processions and music.

- Festa di San Giovanni (June): This is a religious festival celebrating St. John the Baptist.

- Festa di San Giuseppe (March): Celebrate with traditional Italian food, music, and dancing.

- Festa della Madonna della Lettera (July): Celebrate with traditional music, processions, and fireworks.

- Palermo Film Festival (July/August): Enjoy screenings of the latest films from around the world.

- International Puppet Festival (September): Celebrate with puppet shows and performances.

- Festa di Santa Rosalia (September): Celebrate with parades and processions.

- Festa di San Martino (November): Celebrate with traditional foods and music.

Travel Tips

Pack for the weather: Make sure to bring appropriate clothing for the time of year you're visiting. Be sure to pack sunscreen and a hat for the summer months.

Eat local: Sicilian cuisine is famous for its delicious dishes, so be sure to try the local specialties. From arancini to cannoli, Sicily offers a wide variety of mouth-watering dishes.

Take a tour: There are plenty of guided tours available in Sicily, which can help you explore the region and learn more about its history and culture. Some popular tours include food and wine tours, cultural tours, and sightseeing tours.

Be flexible: Sicily is a land of surprises, so be open to exploring and trying new things. You never know what you might discover.

Stay safe: While Sicily is generally safe, it's always important to be aware of your surroundings and follow the rules.

Enjoy yourself: Last but not least, remember to have fun and make the most of the time and amazing memories

Getting There

Getting to Sicily is a delightful experience, one filled with the promise of sun-drenched beaches and cobblestone streets. It is the largest island in the Mediterranean Sea, located south of the mainland of Italy. No matter what your mode of transportation, there are a few key ways to make your way to this beautiful island.

1. Airports

The first way to get to Sicily is by flying. There are several airports scattered around the island, including Falcone-Borsellino Airport in Palermo, Catania-Fontanarossa Airport in Catania, and Vincenzo Florio Airport in Trapani. Depending on your budget and preferred route, you can fly from many major cities in Europe to any of these airports. Plus, the incredible views of the island from the plane are sure to make the journey even more enjoyable.

Flying to Sicily is the quickest way to get to the island, and the views from the plane are indeed stunning. However, it is important to note that flights to Sicily can be expensive, especially during peak tourist season. So, if you're on a tight budget, you may want to consider taking a ferry or renting a car instead.

2. Ferry Services

For those who prefer to travel by sea, ferry services offer a direct route to the island. Ferries sail multiple times a day from mainland Italy to Sicily and vice versa. The journey is usually long, so it is best suited for those who are looking for a more leisurely way to get to the island. Plus, some ferry services offer cabins so you can get a good night's sleep onboard.

while ferries offer a leisurely way to get to Sicily, the journey can be quite long. For example, the ferry from Naples to Palermo takes around 11 hours, while the ferry from Genoa to Palermo takes around 21 hours. It's also worth noting that the length of the journey can be affected by weather conditions, so be sure to check ahead before booking your tickets.

3. Car Rentals

This is a great option if you are looking to explore the island at your own pace. There are several car rental companies in Italy, such as Europcar and Hertz, where you can pick up your vehicle. You can then drive the entire length of the island, from Palermo in the north, to Ragusa in the south. Plus, you can even take a detour to the stunning Aeolian Islands, located in the Tyrrhenian Sea.

it's important to note that driving in Italy can be quite different from driving in other countries. Italian drivers are known for being fast and sometimes aggressive, so be sure to drive carefully and follow local traffic laws. Additionally, some of the roads in Sicily can be quite narrow and winding, so be prepared for some challenging driving conditions.

WHERE TO STAY

Hotels
Popular Hotels in Sicily.

Hotel Villa Carlotta

This hotel is a few minutes' walk from Taormina's center and offers views of the Mediterranean Sea and Mount Etna in the background. It has magnificent rooms and apartments with balconies, as well as a garden with a pool. The Carlotta's air-conditioned rooms, flats, and villas offer a satellite flat-screen TV with a DVD player and an electric kettle. Kitchenettes and dining areas are also included in apartments and villas.

The private bathroom includes a hairdryer and complimentary amenities. Every day, a buffet breakfast is served in the main building, and there is also a bar. The restaurant is open for lunch and supper and provides Sicilian specialties produced with local organic products, as well as a comprehensive wine selection.

San Domenico Palace

A one-of-a-kind establishment, with terraces overlooking mount Etna and Taormina Bay. It has a workout center, a beauty salon, and an outdoor pool. This Taormina luxury hotel is made up of two antique structures. The Garden Wing is a former convent with a cloister from the 15th century.

All rooms are individually designed and include air conditioning and a TV with satellite channels. Most accommodations feature sea views, and some have a private balcony. The hotel's restaurants and bars are mentioned in the most prestigious culinary guides and serve authentic Sicilian cuisine.

.

Algilà Ortigia Charme

Algilà Ortigia Charme is located on Ortigia Island, overlooking the Ionian Sea. It has magnificent, air-conditioned rooms with antique furniture from the 1700s. WiFi is available for free here. It is situated in three buildings from the 1700s that have been adorned with antique furniture and furnishings. Each room has vintage furnishings as well as a separate bathroom with painted tiles. Some rooms have exposed wood beams or a four-poster bed

The restaurant features Mediterranean cuisine, including seafood specialties and gluten-free options. Additional amenities at the facility include free bike rentals and free phone calls to Europe and North America. The Algilà Ortigia Charme Hotel is trekkable from the Cathedral of Siracusa and less than 2km from Castle Maniace.

Villa Belvedere

Villa Belvedere is just a few minutes' walk from the ancient town and stands out against one of eastern Sicily's most spectacular panoramas: the bay of Naxos with its antique coastlines and Mount Etna in the distance. The entire crew is polite, helpful, and honest.

There is also a small parking lot for automobiles. Take advantage of their lovely pool with amazing views. It takes around 10-15 minutes to walk to the main pedestrian areas.

The property features a lift, working air conditioning, and English TV channels.

Throughout the years, despite repeated restorations, the hotel has preserved intact the beautiful beauty of historic residences, adapting to all modern amenities.

The main Villa is available from early April to late November; the Deluxe Studios, Rock Suites, and "Villa Maddalena" Suites are open all year.

The Ashbee

The Ashbee is a subtle adaption of a huge mansion located in beautiful gardens, complete with plenty of marble and ambiance. The bright and airy rooms are simple in design yet have exquisite antique furnishings, and some have patios or terraces overlooking the sea. The panoramic rooftop Terrace Bar serves a wonderful buffet breakfast and cocktails, and more food and drink is offered in a garden bar.

Liberty Hotel

A beautiful villa from the early 1900s that has been restored and converted into a luxury yet intimate hotel with elegant architecture in the center of the city. Its position, which is a stone's throw from Catania's historic and commercial heart, makes it perfect for comfortable business stays or pleasurable vacations. Liberty Hotel has 7 suites, 9 doubles, and 2 singles, each with its own "name" that reflects the mood it conjures. There is a delightful outdoor patio area with a vine-covered canopy that is ideal for breakfast. The rooms are large, with high ceilings and several French doors and the personnel are really kind, helpful, and professional.

Alma Hotel

Alma is a hidden gem in Palermo's historic area. Indeed, it's in a run-down neighborhood, but the interior is bright and contemporary. Choose from one of seven rooms, each with a mural of the ancient city and a breakfast that includes homemade cannoli or cassata. There is no onsite restaurant or bar, although there are several excellent eateries just outside the hotel's doors. This is a great choice for tourists on a minimal budget.

Minareto's Grand Hotel in Syracuse

The Minareto, located on the outskirts of Ortigia on the boundaries of the Plemmirio National Reserve, is a vast complex of rooms, apartments, and villas surrounded by nature. All rooms have patios and are well-equipped, with larger suites offering exclusive access to a sandy beach. There is also a hot tub terrace and sports and spa facilities.

Villa Boscarino

Villa Boscarino is located in Ragusa, 1.5 kilometers from San Giovanni Battista's Church. It has a sun patio and garden views. The on-site bar is available to guests. On-site private parking is free. This hotel's rooms are all air conditioned and include a flat-screen TV with satellite channels. The rooms have a private bathroom with a bath or shower as well as bathrobes. Free toiletries and a hairdryer are provided for your convenience. The whole property at Villa Boscarino has complimentary WiFi. This hotel offers bike and vehicle rental, and the surrounding region is known for horseback riding and hiking.

Monaci della Terra Nere

This stylish environmental sanctuary is located 20 miles from Catania and is great for people who wish to relax by the pool or sea, have a massage, and occasionally hike Mount Etna's slopes. The remodeled 'palmento,' a historic winery with many traditional Sicilian aspects, has been updated with art and designer furnishings. The rooms are lovely, with weathered timbers and lava stone walls, and wood-burning fireplaces, which are essential during the cooler months. If you become hungry, head to the restaurant, which serves seasonal and regional cuisine. It even uses ingredients from the hotel's organic farm, which is a wonderful touch.

Villa Schuler

It is surrounded by huge subtropical gardens and offers panoramic views of Mount Etna and Naxos Bay. The majority of rooms have a furnished balcony or patio. From March to November, the hotel provides mountain bikes and a shuttle service to the beach. The lobby, the cold winter garden, the sun terrace, a botanical garden, and the Palm

Terrace Orangery pavilion are all places to unwind at Hotel Villa Schuler. There is also a TV room, a small library, internet terminals, and a piano area. Guests have the option of booking "room only" or adding breakfast. The hotel is easily accessible by automobile and is one of the few hotels in Taormina's ancient town center that has its own garage with an efficient valet parking service. Breakfast is offered à la carte in the breakfast room, the Orangery, on the patio overlooking the seashore, or directly in the guest rooms.

Calanica

Calanica, located in Cefalù, has a restaurant, an outdoor pool, and a sun deck. Wi-Fi is available for free throughout the hotel. The Calanica's air-conditioned rooms include a garden or sea view and a couch. The private bathroom has complimentary amenities as well as a hairdryer. Every day, a continental breakfast buffet is served, and the à la carte restaurant has sea views. The Madonie Regional Park is about a 20-minute drive away.

Metropole Maison D'Hôtes

The Metropole Maison D'Hôtes, an 18th-century aristocratic mansion, is located in the heart of Taormina. It has breathtaking views of the seaside, beautiful accommodations, and complimentary Wi-Fi. The Metropole Taormina has big en suite rooms, an LCD TV with satelite channels, and air conditioning. Several rooms have views of the sea. The on-site restaurant of the Maison D'Hôtes serves traditional Sicilian cuisine and regional specialties. There is also an outdoor pool and a modest spa center with hammam, hot tub, and massage services.

Casa Talia Modica

Casa Talia blended historic tiles, local stone, and eccentric furnishings to create a hipster refuge in a picturesque Baroque town one hour from Syracuse. The refurbished fishermen's cottages' ten differently built rooms all feature balconies or patios. Superb breakfasts are provided in a rock-hewn dining area, and choices include picnic hampers and treks to local spots where you may enjoy them.

ORTIGIA

WHAT TO SEE AND DO

Must-see Attractions

Sicily offers a wealth of attractions to visitors. From ancient Greek temples to stunning beaches in various towns and cities, explore the top must-see attractions in Sicily.

Palermo:

Palermo, the capital of Sicily, is a vibrant and bustling city with a rich history and culture. The city's architecture reflects the influence of various civilizations that have inhabited the island over the centuries, from the Phoenicians to the Normans. One of the most famous landmarks in the city is the Palazzo dei Normanni, a beautiful example of medieval architecture that houses the Sicilian Regional Assembly. The Cattedrale di Palermo, with its striking blend of Gothic, Baroque, and Norman styles, is also a must-see attraction.

The city is also known for its lively street life and colorful markets. The Ballarò Market is a great place to experience the local culture and cuisine, with vendors selling everything from fresh produce to street food. The city is also famous for its nightlife, with numerous bars and clubs catering to all tastes.

Agrigento:

Agrigento, located on the south coast of Sicily, is home to the Valley of the Temples, a UNESCO World Heritage Site. The site consists of a number of well-preserved ancient Greek temples, including the Temple of Concordia, the Temple of Juno, and the Temple of Hercules. The temples date back to the 5th century BC and are considered some of the finest examples of Greek architecture in the world.

In addition to the Valley of the Temples, Agrigento has many other notable attractions, such as the Cathedral of Agrigento, which is built in the Baroque style, and the

Sanctuary of the Madonna of the Rosary, which dates back to the 17th century. The city is also known for its stunning beaches, such as Scala dei Turchi, which features distinctive white limestone cliffs.

Taormina:

Taormina, a charming town on the east coast of Sicily, is famous for its stunning views of the Ionian Sea and its ancient Greek theatre. The theatre, which dates back to the 3rd century BC, is one of the most important archaeological sites in the region. The town's picturesque beaches and vibrant nightlife make it a popular destination for tourists.

Visitors to Taormina should also check out the Palazzo Corvaja, a beautiful Gothic-Renaissance palace that now houses the town's tourist office, and the 13th-century Cathedral of San Nicolò. The town is also famous for its cuisine, with many restaurants serving traditional Sicilian dishes such as pasta alla norma and cassata siciliana.

Etna:

Mount Etna, located on the east coast of Sicily, is one of the most active volcanoes in the world. Visitors can take guided tours of the volcano, explore its many trails and paths, and even take a cable car to the summit. The volcano is home to a variety of unique wildlife, including the Sicilian shrew and the Etna birch mouse.

In addition to its natural attractions, Etna also boasts a number of excellent restaurants and bars. Visitors can sample local wines, such as Etna Rosso and Bianco, and try traditional dishes such as pasta alla norma and arancini

Catania:

Located on the eastern coast of Sicily, Catania is a city that seamlessly blends the old with the new. Here, visitors can stroll through bustling streets lined with vendors selling fresh produce and artisan crafts, while catching glimpses of historic landmarks like the Cathedral of Catania and the castle of Ursino. And when the sun goes down, the city really comes alive, with lively bars and restaurants offering everything from classic Sicilian dishes to international cuisine.

The city is also home to some stunning natural attractions, like the imposing Mount Etna, an active volcano that dominates the skyline. Visitors can hike through its rugged terrain, or simply admire it from afar. And with its proximity to the Mediterranean Sea, Catania also boasts some beautiful beaches where visitors can soak up the sun and enjoy the crystal-clear waters.

Syracuse:

Nestled on the eastern coast of Sicily, Syracuse is a city that has played an important role in Mediterranean history for centuries. Here, visitors can explore ancient ruins like the Temple of Apollo and the Cathedral of Syracuse, marvel at the intricate architecture of the city's many churches and palaces, or take a stroll through the bustling markets that line the streets.

. It's also a vibrant and modern place, with a bustling street life and a thriving food scene. Visitors can sample traditional Sicilian dishes like arancini (fried rice balls) and cannoli (sweet pastry filled with ricotta cheese), or try international flavors at one of the city's many restaurants and cafes.

No trip to Syracuse would be complete without taking in the stunning views of the Mediterranean Sea. Visitors can wander along the city's picturesque waterfront, relax on one of its many beaches, or take a boat tour to explore the nearby islands.

Marsala:

Marsala is a city that is famous for its rich winemaking heritage. Tourist can explore the city's many vineyards, learn about the history and culture of wine production in the region, and of course, enjoy some of the delicious local wines.

The city is also home to a wealth of historic attractions, including the Church of San Pietro and the Palazzo Municipale. And with its picturesque streets and stunning Mediterranean views, Marsala is a city that truly embodies the beauty of southern Italy.

With its proximity to the coast, there are plenty of opportunities to enjoy the sea as well, whether it's lounging on one of the city's many beaches or taking a boat tour to explore the nearby islands.

Erice:

Perched atop a hill on the western coast of Sicily, Erice is a town that offers visitors breathtaking views of the Mediterranean Sea and a glimpse into Sicily's rich cultural heritage. Visitors can explore ancient landmarks like the Castle of Erice and the Church of San Giuliano, marvel at the intricate architecture of the town's many palaces and churches, or simply wander through its picturesque streets and soak up the local atmosphere.

Ragusa:

Ragusa is known for its rich history, stunning architecture, and picturesque landscapes. One of the most significant features of Ragusa is its division into two parts, Ragusa Superiore and Ragusa Ibla.

Ragusa Superiore is the more modern section of the city and is characterized by its long main boulevard, Corso Italia. The boulevard is considered one of Ragusa's best promenades and offers stunning views of the surrounding landscape.

Ragusa Ibla, on the other hand, is the ancient heart of the city and is known for its rich history and stunning architecture. The most picturesque way to approach Ragusa Ibla is by using the Santa Maria delle Scale, a long set of stairs that descends from Ragusa Superiore to the medieval heart of Ibla.

One of the must-see attractions in Ragusa is the Giardino Ibleo, a beautiful public garden that offers breathtaking views of the Irminio Valley. The garden also houses several religious structures, including the Church of San Giacomo, which is well worth a visit.

CEFALU

Shopping in Sicily

Sicily is a haven for shoppers looking for a unique and unforgettable shopping experience. It has a diverse array of shopping options, ranging from luxury boutiques to local markets and specialty shops.

Here are some of the top shopping experiences in Sicily:

1. Palermo's Markets: Palermo is a shopper's paradise, with some of the most bustling and vibrant markets in all of Italy. From the Ballarò in the old town to the nearby Vucciria and Capo markets, Palermo's markets offer a glimpse into the heart of the city's local culture. Visitors can browse through the stalls selling everything from fresh produce and seafood to meat, cheese, and handmade goods.

2. Catania's Shopping Streets: Catania is another great shopping destination in Sicily, with upscale shopping streets that cater to the luxury shopper. Stroll down Via Etnea and Via Crociferi to discover

designer boutiques, jewelry stores, and other high-end shops.

3. Sicilian Specialty Stores: For those looking for unique and one-of-a-kind souvenirs, Sicily's specialty stores are a must-visit. Stop by Trapani for some of the finest handmade jewelry and check out the island's renowned ceramics shops for a stunning piece of Italian art.

4. Local Food Markets: To truly experience the flavors of Sicily, visit one of the many local food markets scattered throughout the island. From the famous Vucciria Market in Palermo to the bustling markets in Catania, visitors can find an abundance of fresh fruits and vegetables, local cheeses, olive oil, and other culinary delights.

5. Catania's Fish Markets: Catania is renowned for its fresh seafood, and its fish markets are a testament to this. Get there early in the morning to find the freshest catch of the day and take home some of the island's most prized seafood.

Best Places to Shop

Sicilia Outlet Village - a retail center near Agira on the A19 with high-end designer boutiques such as Gucci, Prada, Dolce & Gabbana, and Armani, as well as other accessible brands such as Pandora, Nike, and Vans. The shopping experience is completed with charging stations for electric cars, ATMs, personal shoppers, concierge services, and shipping options.

Mercatino delle Pulci - a monthly flea market held in Modica on the last Sunday of the month. The market offers a range of secondhand products, including antique collectibles, used furniture, ancient records, jewelry, and vintage Caltagirone pottery.

Etnapolis - a megamall in Belpasso, about 14 kilometers northwest of Catania, that houses numerous well-known fashion and lifestyle brands such as H&M, JD Sports, Pull & Bear, Sisley, Benetton, and Zara. The mall also features several restaurants, cafes, fast-food establishments, a multiplex theater, and over 6,000 parking spots, free Wi-Fi, and a dog walking area.

Antica Dolceria Bonajuto - Sicily's oldest chocolate manufacturer in Modica. The shop offers chocolate bars and classic Sicilian sweet delights like cannoli, cassatine, nucatoli, m'pagnuccata, and mpanatigghi. Visitors can learn about the shop's history and how the delicacies are prepared by joining one of the regular Fattojo Bonajuto trips.

Corso Italia - a bustling boulevard in Catania with one of the greatest collections of upscale retail stores on the island. Both sides of the street feature well-known chain retailers and high-end designer outlets such as Stefanel, Tommy Hilfiger, Guess, Max Mara, Boss, and Benetton, as well as local designer names like Elisabetta Franchi and Chiara B.

Mercato del Capo - one of the oldest marketplaces in Palermo, Sicily, located on Via Sant'Agostino. The market sells meat, fish, fruits, and vegetables, and is popular with both locals and tourists. Visitors can people-watch, shop, and eat street cuisine.

Magazzini Anita - a well-known fashion boutique in Palermo that specializes in vintage apparel from the 1920s to the 1980s. The store offers unique clothing, purses, and jewelry at reasonable costs for fashionistas searching for something a little unusual.

Ceramiche Artistiche Carco di Irene Cabibbo - a ceramic shop in Caltagirone, known as the "City of Sicilian Ceramics." The shop offers distinctive native pottery that layers a restricted palette of yellows, greens, and blues over a white backdrop, and features a Majolica nativity scene that serves as the centerpiece of a modest exhibition of work.

Mercato Ballaro - an open-air market in Palermo that predominantly offers food, such as locally supplied fish, vegetables, meat, cheese, spices, and bread. Visitors can watch as merchants neatly display their products and buy some of the best food in Sicily.

Santo Stefano di Camastra - a town on the north coast of Sicily, halfway between Palermo and Messina. It is widely recognized for its ceramics legacy and has a plethora of firms that create and sell various clay goods.

La Giara - founded in 1953 by the Patti family, is one of the oldest. They still handcraft colorful bowls, bottles, vases, and trademark Majolica tiles. If you want a genuine memento, shop carefully because several goods for sale in town are mass-produced.

Dining In Sicily

Dining in Sicily is a unique culinary experience that blends the best of Italian and Mediterranean cuisine with a rich history and cultural heritage. Sicilian cuisine is known for its bold flavors, fresh ingredients, and hearty portions that are sure to satisfy even the most discerning palate.

One of the most distinctive features of Sicilian cuisine is its use of fresh, locally sourced ingredients. From seafood and vegetables to citrus fruits and nuts, Sicilian cuisine is renowned for its vibrant colors and bold flavors that come from the island's fertile soils and sunny climate. Fresh seafood, such as swordfish, tuna, and sardines, is a staple in Sicilian cuisine and can be prepared in a variety of ways, including grilled, fried, or baked.

Sicilian cuisine is also famous for its pasta dishes, which range from simple tomato-based sauces to more complex dishes like pasta alla norma, which features eggplant, tomato sauce, and ricotta cheese. The island's cuisine is heavily influenced by its Arab, Greek, and Spanish heritage, resulting in a unique blend of flavors and ingredients that are unlike any other Italian region.

Dining in Sicily is deeply connected to the island's history and traditions. Many Sicilian dishes have been passed down for generations, and each recipe tells a story about the region's cultural heritage. For example, arancini, a popular Sicilian street food, is a deep-fried rice ball that is traditionally filled with meat sauce, peas, and mozzarella cheese. This dish has roots in the Arab occupation of Sicily in the 9th century and has since become a beloved staple of the island's cuisine.

Another example is cassata, a traditional Sicilian dessert that is made with sponge cake, ricotta cheese, and candied fruit. This dessert has been a fixture of Sicilian cuisine since the 17th century and is often served during special occasions, such as weddings and religious celebrations.

When dining in Sicily, it's not just about the food, but also the atmosphere and hospitality. Sicilians are known for their warm and welcoming nature, and this extends to their dining traditions. Many restaurants in Sicily offer a family-style dining experience, where guests can share a variety of dishes and enjoy a leisurely meal with loved ones. This dining style is a reflection of the island's strong sense of community and is a testament to the importance of food in Sicilian culture.

Best Sicilian dishes to try

Arancini: They are deep-fried rice balls filled with ragù sauce, peas, and cheese, then covered in breadcrumbs. They are a popular street snack and appetizer in Sicily.

Spaghetti alla Norma: This is a famous Sicilian pasta dish prepared with eggplant, tomatoes, garlic, and ricotta salata cheese. The name "Norma" is claimed to have derived from a great opera by Bellini, who was born in Catania.

Caponata: A sweet and sour stew cooked with eggplant, celery, onions, tomatoes, capers, and olives. It may be served as a side dish or a vegetarian main entrée.

Sarde a Beccafico: This is a stuffed sardine dish packed with breadcrumbs, pine nuts, raisins, and parsley, then cooked in the oven. It is a typical Sicilian meal prepared on special occasions.

Pasta con le Sarde: A pasta dish prepared with sardines, fennel, onions, pine nuts, raisins, and saffron. It is a classic dish from Palermo.

Polpo alla Luciana: A stew cooked with octopus, tomatoes, garlic, and chili pepper. It is a popular meal in the coastal parts of Sicily.

Involtini di Melanzane: They are eggplant buns stuffed with cheese, breadcrumbs, and parsley, then cooked in the oven. They are a traditional Sicilian appetizer or side dish.

Pesce Spada alla Messinese: A swordfish dish prepared with tomatoes, onions, capers, and olives. It is a speciality of the city of Messina.

Scaccia Ragusana: A filled flatbread cooked with tomato sauce, cheese, and local sausage. It is a classic street snack from Ragusa.

Pasta con le Fave: A spaghetti dish cooked with fava beans, wild fennel, and pecorino cheese. It is a classic Sicilian meal eaten in the spring.

Sfincione: A typical Sicilian pizza prepared with a thick and fluffy dough, topped with tomato sauce, onions, anchovies, and breadcrumbs. It is often consumed as a snack or as a light supper.

Pesto Trapanese: A pesto sauce composed with almonds, tomatoes, garlic, and basil. It is a speciality of Trapani, a city on the western coast of Sicily. The sauce is generally served with pasta or as a topping for bruschetta. The inclusion of almonds instead of pine nuts, which are more typically used in classic Italian pesto, is a distinguishing element of this Sicilian sauce.

Fritto Misto di Mare: A mixed seafood fry prepared with squid, shrimp, sardines, and other shellfish. It is a classic meal in coastal areas and served as a starter or a main entrée.

Brioche Con Gelato: A Sicilian dish prepared with a brioche bun filled with gelato. It is a popular street dish and a pleasant treat on hot summer days.

Cannoli: A pastry created with a fried dough shell filled with sweet ricotta cheese, candied fruit, and chocolate chips. It is a classic Sicilian dessert.

Cassata Siciliana: A tiered sponge cake filled with delicious ricotta cheese, candied fruit, and marzipan. It is a typical dessert offered on special occasions.

Cassatella Di Sant'Agata: A miniature variant of the cassata, shaped like a half-moon and filled with sweet ricotta cheese and chocolate chips. It is a speciality of Catania.

Granita Siciliana: A shaved ice dessert created with fruit syrup, such as lemon, strawberry, or almond. It is a delicious dessert enjoyed across Sicily.

Frutta Martorana: A classic Sicilian delicacy prepared with almond paste formed into fruits and embellished with vibrant colors. It is a speciality of Palermo.

Panelle: A chickpea fritter sandwich prepared with fried chickpea flour patties, lemon, and parsley. It is a popular street snack in Paler

Restaurants to Visit in Sicily

Gourmet 32

Gourmet 32 is a popular place for Sicilian specialties in Taormina. Its culinary brigade tackles traditional Sicilian food and changes them with a contemporary twist. Try the duck breast grilled with a Sicilian citrus sauce or the local swordfish with capers and olives. You can finish off with an almond parfait or a delectable tiramisu.

Dine on the covered patio if you can for excellent views and atmosphere. Gourmet 32 is hidden in an alley east of Teatro Antico di Taormina, a famous Greco-Roman amphitheatre.

Location: Via Bagnoli Croci, 31, 98039 Taormina ME, Italy

Otto Geleng

Otto Geleng, named after the German painter who was drawn to Taormina, is a famous Sicilian restaurant located on the terrace of the Grand Hotel Timeo, a luxury Belmond hotel. The chef uses locally sourced ingredients from both land and sea to create classic Mediterranean cuisine with a contemporary twist.

Otto Geleng's menu includes tuna belly with cooked must and seasoned cabbage, ravioli with caviar and porcini mushrooms, and red mullet with artichokes, foie gras and passion fruit.

Location: Via Teatro Greco, 59, 98039 Taormina ME, Italy

La Madia

La Madia is a restaurant located in Licata, a town situated on the south coast of Sicily. It has received two Michelin stars, and its chef serves unique and exquisite Sicilian cuisine. The restaurant has a contemporary and sophisticated dining room with a minimalist decor that emphasizes the meal.

The chef's special ingredient is adding a local touch to each dish, allowing the patrons to experience the essence of the island. La Madia's a la carte menu includes items such as smoked cod and honey-glazed pigeon, as well as several tasting menus for those who want to try an assortment of dishes.

Location: Corso Filippo Re Capriata, 22, 92027 Licata AG, Italy

Viri Ku C'e

Viri Ku C'e is a riverbank dining place in Vittoria in southern Sicily. It's right across the street from Scoglitti's sandy beach, making it a perfect spot to appreciate seafood after a day in the water. Foods on the set price menu change daily, dependent on what's been caught.

You may start with clams, oysters, mussels, scallops, langoustines and shrimp, followed by homemade pasta and complete, grilled fish filleted for you at the table.

Location: Via Riviera Gela , 13/a, 97019 Scoglitti, Vittoria, RG, Italy

Osteria Da Rita

Osteria Da Rita is a classic Sicilian restaurant in Taormina delivering great dishes in abundant portions. It's nestled along a quiet street, making it a treat to dine outside at one of the tables, which wear gorgeous red gingham tablecloths.

The dish is uniquely Sicilian, as is the wine accompanying it. You may find an extensive choice of fundamental favorites at Osteria Da Rita. The atmosphere's friendly and laidback. Clients are welcomed with open arms and permitted to choose the music and join the singing.

Location: Via Calapitrulli, 3, 98039 Taormina ME, Italy

Duomo Ristorante

Duomo Ristorante is a two Michelin-starred restaurant situated in Ragusa, and it derives its name from the nearby San Giorgio Cathedral. It is known for its innovative and unique take on classic Sicilian dishes. The restaurant has a mesmerizing view of the city and offers an unforgettable culinary experience.

The restaurant's chef reimagines the classics, using three essential ingredients in every meal: oil, wheat, and salt. Duomo's specialties include the fish of the day or crispy fried tuna with honey as starters and macaroni with fried eggplant and Florentine sirloin steak as main courses.

Location: Ibla, Via Capitano Bocchieri, 31, 97100 Ragusa RG, Italy

Manna Noto

Manna Noto is a restaurant in Noto that gives a feast for the senses with its Mediterranean food and ambient setting. Step inside to find a stunning environment illuminated with statement lighting and equipped with distinctive decorations.

Standouts include a room divider of wine bottles and an illuminated soda sign over the bar. The attractive, contemporary design replaces a space that was formerly the ground floor of a palace.

Savor a fresh orange salad, a Sicilian delicacy, or some grilled fish. Manna Noto's handmade pasta is highly regarded.

Location: Via Rocco Pirri, 19, 96017 Noto SR, Italy

La Capinera

La Capinera is another Michelin-starred restaurant in Taormina that offers a simple and excellent fine dining experience.

La Capinera's menu includes warm pistachio cake and orange mousse, mortadella-stuffed baby calamari, paccheri pasta sautéed with clams and shrimps, and slow-roasted lamb in a Marsala wine sauce. In the summer, guests can dine on the terrace with a view of the Ionian Sea, while during the colder months; they can enjoy a meal in the small dining room.

Location: Via Nazionale, 177, 98039 Taormina ME, Italy

I Pupi

I Pupi, located in Bagheria, is a Michelin-starred restaurant that draws inspiration from Sicily's street culinary scene, ancient family traditions, and the island's bountiful native produce. The decor is simple and monochrome, and the dishes are exquisitely prepared and bursting with flavor.

I Pupi's menu includes a variation on the traditional Sicilian stigghiola, made with tuna and squid instead of lamb and leeks.

Location: Via del Cavaliere, 59, 90011 Bagheria PA, Italy

Osteria Ballarò

Osteria Ballarò is a restaurant in Palermo that honors the slow food movement and occupies the former stables of the old Palace Cattolica. The restaurant's stunning decor includes exposed brick walls and a magnificent vaulted ceiling.

All the meat, seafood, cheese, and wine come from Sicily, with most purchased from local artisan vendors. The fruit is also fully seasonal, so the menu changes regularly. Osteria Ballarò's menu features handmade pasta tortelloni with buffalo ricotta cheese and tenerumi (Sicilian broadleaf vegetables), among other dishes.

Location: Via Calascibetta, 25, 90133 Palermo PA, Italy

Wine Tasting In Sicily

No discussion of dining in Sicily would be complete without mentioning the wine. Sicily is home to some of the world's oldest vineyards, and its wines are highly prized for their rich and complex flavors. From the crisp and refreshing white wines of the island's north coast to the bold and robust reds of the interior, Sicilian wines are the perfect accompaniment to any meal.

Sicilian wine has a long and fascinating history, dating back to ancient times. The Greeks were the first to introduce wine to the island, and they quickly realized that Sicily's warm and sunny climate, along with its fertile soil, was ideal for wine production. Over the centuries, many different cultures have left their mark on Sicily, and each has contributed to the island's winemaking traditions.

Today, Sicily is the largest wine-producing region in Italy, with over 100,000 hectares of vineyards. The island is particularly well-known for its red wines, which are made from the Nero d'Avola grape, but it also produces a wide variety of other wines, including white, rosé, and dessert wines.

The Best Wineries to Visit in Sicily

If you're planning a wine-tasting tour in Sicily, there are many wineries to choose from. Here are some of the best

Planeta Winery

Planeta Winery is one of the most well-known and respected wineries in Sicily. The winery was founded in

1995 by the Planeta family, who has been making wine in Sicily for over 300 years. Planeta Winery has several vineyards throughout the island and produces a wide range of high-quality wines.

Gambino Vini

Set on the slopes of Mount Etna, Gambino Vini is a family-owned winery that produces a variety of wines, including red, white, and rosé wines.

Azienda Agricola Augustali

This winery is situated in the countryside near Siracusa and is recognized for producing organic wines produced from local grape varietals.

Emilio Sciacca

This winery is situated near the town of Marsala and is famed for its Marsala wines, a fortified wine that is a speciality of the area.

Terra Costantino

Terra Costantino is a family-run winery in the village of Valguarnera Caropepe and makes wines produced from local grape varietals, including Nero d'Avola and Grillo.

Scilio - Etna Wines since 1815

Scilio is one of the oldest wineries in the area and is noted for making high-quality wines using traditional techniques.

Cantina Cambria Vini

This winery in the town of Noto churns out a sophisticated variety of wines, including Nero d'Avola, Syrah, and Chardonnay.

Etna Urban Winery

Standing tall in the center of Catania, Etna Urban winery is noted for its unique approach to winemaking and produces a variety of wines utilizing grapes from Mount Etna.

Vigna di Pettineo

As a pride of Castiglione di Sicilia, Vigna di Pettineo offers a variety of wines derived from local grape varietals, including Nerello Mascalese and Carricante.

Donnafugata Winery

Donnafugata Winery is another popular destination for wine lovers in Sicily. The winery was founded in 1983 and is known for its innovative approach to winemaking. Donnafugata produces a wide variety of wines, including varieties like Chardonnay and Cabernet Sauvignon.

Tasca d'Almerita Winery

Tasca d'Almerita Winery is a family-owned winery that has been making wine in Sicily for over 200 years. The winery has several vineyards throughout the island and produces both traditional Sicilian varieties and international varieties.

What to Expect on a Wine-Tasting Tour in Sicily

Vineyard Tour

Most wine-tasting tours in Sicily will start with a tour of the vineyards. You'll have the opportunity to see the grapes up close and learn about the different varieties that are grown in the region. Your guide will also explain the terroir and climate conditions that make Sicilian wine so unique.

Winery Tour

After the vineyard tour, you'll visit the winery itself, where you'll learn about the winemaking process. You'll see the barrels where the wine is aged, the bottling process, and the cellars where the wine is stored. Your guide will explain the different steps in the winemaking process, from harvesting the grapes to fermenting the juice and aging the wine.

Wine Tasting

The highlight of any wine-tasting tour is, of course, the wine tasting itself. You'll have the opportunity to taste several different wines produced by the winery, and your guide will explain the tasting notes and characteristics of each wine. You'll learn about the different grape varieties, the aging process, and the different factors that influence the flavor of the wine.

Food Pairing

Wine tasting in Sicily is often accompanied by delicious local food, such as cheeses, cured meats, olives, and bread. Your guide will explain the art of food pairing, and you'll learn how to pair different wines with different foods to enhance the flavors of both.

Buying Wine At the end of the wine-tasting tour, you'll have the opportunity to buy some of the wines you've tasted. Many wineries in Sicily offer a range of different wines, from affordable everyday wines to more expensive reserve bottles. Your guide will be able to advise you on the best wines to buy based on your taste preferences and budget.

SICILIAN ADVENTURES

Outdoor Activities

Hiking

Hiking in Sicily can take you to a variety of terrains, each with its own unique charm. The island's most famous hiking destination is the Mount Etna, the tallest active volcano in Europe. Hiking up to the summit of this majestic mountain is a truly unforgettable experience, with breathtaking views of the surrounding landscape and the thrill of being close to the heart of one of the earth's most powerful natural phenomena.

There are many hiking routes up to the summit of Mount Etna, ranging from easy to difficult, so hikers of all levels can find a suitable path. Along the way, you can encounter unique flora and fauna, such as the black lava rock formations, and the rare and endangered Silene aetnensis plant.

Another popular hiking destination in Sicily is the Nebrodi Mountains. These mountains cover a vast area in the northeast of the island and offer an excellent opportunity for hikers to explore the island's unspoiled wilderness. The Nebrodi Mountains boast a rich biodiversity, with a variety of plant and animal species that can only be found in this area. The hiking trails here are well marked and offer a range of difficulties, from easy walks to challenging treks that require a good level of fitness.

The Madonie Mountains, located in the north-central part of Sicily, is another stunning destination for hiking enthusiasts. This mountain range is known for its jagged peaks, deep valleys, and rolling hills, which offer a variety of hiking experiences. Hikers can explore the picturesque villages nestled in the valleys, such as Castelbuono and Polizzi Generosa, or take on the challenging trails that lead to the highest peaks. The Madonie Mountains are also home to a diverse range of flora and fauna, including the Sicilian fir, which can only be found here.

For those who prefer coastal hikes, Sicily offers a plethora of options. The island's coastline stretches over 1000 km, with many pristine beaches, hidden coves, and rocky cliffs waiting to be discovered. The Zingaro Nature Reserve, located on the northwest coast of Sicily, is a popular destination for hikers and nature lovers. The reserve covers an area of 1650 hectares and offers a range of hiking trails that wind their way through the park's stunning landscape, including steep cliffs, hidden beaches, and turquoise waters. Hikers can also encounter a variety of wildlife, including the Audouin's gull, peregrine falcon, and loggerhead sea turtle.

Sicily's Aeolian Islands, located off the northeast coast of the island, are also a popular destination for hikers looking for a coastal adventure. The islands boast a unique landscape, with active volcanoes, black sand beaches, and crystal-clear waters. The islands' hiking trails offer stunning views of the Mediterranean Sea and the surrounding islands. One of the most popular hiking trails in the Aeolian Islands is the trail that leads to the summit of the Stromboli volcano, which offers a unique opportunity to witness the eruption of the volcano's fiery lava.

Scuba Diving

Scuba diving is a thrilling and exciting outdoor activity that allows individuals to explore the underwater world. Sicily, an island located in the Mediterranean Sea, is a popular destination for scuba diving enthusiasts due to its crystal clear waters, colorful marine life, and stunning underwater landscapes,.

Best Dive Sites in Sicily

Sicily has a wide variety of dive sites that cater to both beginners and experienced divers. Here are some of the best dive sites in Sicily:

Isola delle Correnti

Isola delle Correnti is a small island located at the southern tip of Sicily. The dive site is known for its strong currents, which can be challenging for beginners but offer an exhilarating experience for experienced divers. The site is home to a variety of marine life, including octopuses, moray eels, and schools of fish.

Punta Braccetto

Punta Braccetto is a dive site located on the southeast coast of Sicily. The site features a rocky reef that is home to a variety of marine life, including lobsters, sea urchins, and schools of fish. The site is also home to a sunken shipwreck for in depth exploration..

Zingaro Nature Reserve

The Zingaro Nature Reserve is a protected area located on the northwest coast of Sicily. The reserve features a variety of dive sites that cater to all levels of divers.. The reserve also features underwater caves and tunnels that can be explored by experienced divers.

Ustica Island

Ustica Island is a small island located off the coast of Sicily. The island is a popular dive site due to its crystal clear waters and stunning underwater landscapes. The site is home to a variety of marine life, including barracudas, groupers, and corals.

Scopello

Scopello is a small village located on the northwest coast of Sicily. The village is home to a dive site known as the Tonnara di Scopello, which is a sunken tuna factory that has become a popular dive site due to its unique architecture and stunning underwater scenery.

Taormina

Taormina is home to a dive site known as the Isola Bella, which is a small island located just off the coast.It houses octopuses, sea urchins, and colorful coral formations.

Grotta Azzurra

Grotta Azzurra, also known as the Blue Grotto, is a sea cave located on the east coast of Sicily. The cave is known for its stunning blue waters and is accessible only by boat. The cave offers a unique diving experience as divers can explore the underwater cave system and see the stunning blue colors of the water.

Horseback Riding

The island is home to several equestrian centers and ranches that offer horseback riding tours for riders of all levels of experience. These tours can range from leisurely rides through picturesque countryside to more challenging adventures through rugged terrain.

One of the most popular horseback riding tours in Sicily is the Madonie Park tour, which takes riders through the stunning Madonie Mountains. The tour offers riders breathtaking views of the surrounding landscape, including rolling hills, verdant forests, and quaint medieval villages.

The Madonie Mountains are also home to a diverse range of flora and fauna, providing riders with a unique opportunity to observe the island's wildlife up close. Riders can spot everything from wild boars and foxes to majestic eagles soaring through the skies.

The tour also offers riders the chance to visit several historic sites, including the ruins of ancient Greek and Roman settlements, as well as stunning medieval churches and castles. These sites offer a glimpse into Sicily's rich history and culture, providing riders with a unique educational experience.

For those looking for a more challenging ride, the Etna Park tour offers riders a thrilling adventure through the rugged terrain surrounding Mount Etna, one of the world's most active volcanoes. The tour takes riders through rocky trails and steep inclines, offering a true test of skill and endurance.

Along the way, riders can enjoy breathtaking views of the surrounding countryside, including stunning vistas of the volcanic landscape and distant coastal towns. The tour also offers riders the chance to explore ancient lava caves and craters, providing a unique insight into the geology of the region.

For those with less experience, there are several beginner-friendly tours available that offer a more leisurely pace and gentler terrain. These tours take riders through scenic countryside and charming rural villages, providing a relaxing and enjoyable ride for riders of all ages.

Horseback riding in Sicily offers riders a unique opportunity to explore the island's stunning natural beauty and rich cultural heritage. Whether you're a seasoned rider looking for a thrilling adventure or a beginner looking for a relaxing ride, Sicily's equestrian centers and ranches have something to deliver.

Some Horseback Riding Tours In Sicily

La Pineta Ranch - Situated in Castellammare del Golfo, this ranch provides guided horseback riding experiences in the picturesque Zingaro Reserve natural park.

Sicily Horse Riding - This riding facility is situated in Nicolosi, close to Mount Etna. They provide trips ranging from short rides to full-day excursions that let people to experience the magnificent terrain of the volcano and neighboring regions.

Ranch Capo Grecale - This ranch provides excursions of southern Sicily's magnificent beaches and gorgeous scenery.

Horse Country Resort Congress & Spa - Situated in Arborea, this resort provides horseback riding trips across western Sicily's stunning natural settings.

Ippovia - This riding facility in San Vito Lo Capo, offers excursions of the gorgeous coastline and neighboring regions of northern Sicily.

Villa Favorita Horse Country Resort - This Marsala resort provides horseback riding experiences through western Sicily's picturesque countryside and wineries.

Centro Ippico San Lorenzo – Esconced in Ragusa, it provides trips through the lovely landscape of southern Sicily.

Mountain Biking

Mountain riding in Sicily is a terrific way to see the breathtaking nature of this lovely Italian island. From the rough coastline of the Ionian Sea to the undulating hills of the interior, there is something for all abilities of mountain bikers. Sicily provides a range of terrain, ranging from moderate woodland trails to challenging single track and steep descents. In addition to the beautiful scenery, mountain bikers may visit the historic sites and quaint communities that dot the island.

Madonie National Park:

The Madonie National Park Trail starts in Polizzi Generosa and takes you into the spectacular Madonie Mountains, passing through charming villages, wooded areas, and scenic panoramas.

Nebrodi Mountains: The Nebrodi Mountains Path winds through the Nebrodi Mountains' rugged terrain, through ancient woodlands, abandoned communities, and breathtaking views.

Mount Etna Trail: This path goes to the peak of the famous Mount Etna volcano, from where you may enjoy stunning views of the island and the surrounding sea.

Alcantara Gorges Trail: This trail runs through the magnificent Alcantara Gorges, where you may ride beside the river and take in the scenery.

Cava dei Servi Trail: This hike travels through the scenic Cava dei Servi natural reserve, passing through forests and along the banks of a beautiful river.

Monte Bonifato: The Monte Bonifato Trail ascends Mount Bonifato's upper slopes, affording panoramic views of the surrounding environment and the sea.

Pantalica Necropolis Trail: This route takes you through the ancient ruins of Pantalica, a UNESCO World Heritage site where you may explore the ruins of an ancient city while riding through stunning countryside.

The Mount San Calogero Path ascends Mt San Calogero's steep slopes, passing through woodlands and affording stunning views of the Mediterranean Sea.

Way through the beautiful Zingaro Nature Reserve: This path takes you through the magnificent Zingaro Nature Reserve, where you may ride along the beach and enjoy wonderful sea views.

Vendicari Natural Reserve: Cycle through the spectacular Vendicari Natural Reserve, where you may see a variety of wildlife, including flamingos and sea turtles, as you ride through marshes, forests, and along the beach.

Cultural Experiences

Sicily is a cultural paradise, offering something for everyone. From its world-class museums to its vibrant festivals and historic sites, this island is a treasure trove of cultural experiences waiting to be explored.

Museums

Sicily is home to some of the world's most fascinating museums, offering a glimpse into the island's vibrant past. The most notable of these museums is the Museo Archeologico Regionale di Palermo, which houses a vast collection of artifacts dating back to the prehistoric era. From ancient pottery to intricate mosaics, this museum is a treasure trove of historical relics that showcase the island's diverse cultural influences.

If you're a fan of art, be sure to visit the Galleria Regionale della Sicilia, which features an impressive collection of Renaissance and Baroque paintings, including works by Caravaggio, Antonello da Messina, and other Italian masters. The Museo del Tesoro di San Lorenzo is another must-visit for art enthusiasts, as it houses an exquisite collection of silverware and goldwork dating back to the 13th century.

Museums worth a visit

Museo Archeologico Regionale Paolo Orsi (Syracuse) - One of the most prominent archaeological museums in Italy, it has a great collection of ancient objects from prehistoric periods to the Roman era.

Museo Salinas (Palermo) - Housed in a former monastery, this museum showcases a broad variety of antiquities from the ancient Greek and Roman eras, as well as medieval and contemporary art.

Museo Regionale Pepoli (Trapani) - This museum is devoted to the history and culture of the city of Trapani and the surrounding area. It contains exhibitions on art, archaeology, and anthropology.

Museo Archeologico di Aidone (Enna) - Situated in the heart of Sicily, this museum exhibits an extraordinary collection of relics from the ancient city of Morgantina, including Greek pottery and Roman sculpture.

Museo Regionale di Messina (Messina) - This museum exhibits collections of art and archaeology from the Greek, Roman, and Byzantine eras, as well as medieval and contemporary art.

Museo Civico Castle Ursino (Catania) - Housed in a medieval castle, this museum contains exhibits on the history and culture of Catania and the surrounding area, including ancient antiquities and medieval art.

Museo Civico di Palazzo Bellomo (Syracuse) - This museum is built in a former palace and displays exhibitions on the art and history of Syracuse, including medieval and Renaissance artworks.

Museo Diocesano (Palermo) - Situated in the heart of Palermo's historic city, this museum offers exhibitions on the art and history of the Catholic Church in Sicily, including religious items and paintings.

Museo Regionale di Palazzo D'Aumale (Terrasini) - This museum is set in a splendid 18th-century palace and has exhibits on the art and history of western Sicily, including medieval and Renaissance art.

Museo Whitaker (Marsala) - Situated in a 19th-century wine warehouse, this museum contains exhibits on the history and culture of western Sicily, including ancient antiquities and local crafts.

Festivals

Sicily is famous for its colorful festivals, which celebrate everything from the island's patron saints to its world-renowned cuisine. The most famous of these festivals is the Feast of Saint Agatha, which takes place in Catania every February. This festival is a lively affair, featuring parades, fireworks, and traditional Sicilian music and dance. Another popular festival is the Infiorata di Noto, which takes place in May and sees the streets of Noto adorned with intricate floral designs.

If you're a foodie, you won't want to miss the Targa Florio Vintage Car Rally, which takes place in May and features classic cars driving through some of Sicily's most picturesque towns and villages. And for those who love music, the Festival della Valle d'Itria is a must-visit, featuring world-class opera performances set against the stunning backdrop of the Valle d'Itria.

Historic Sites

Sicily is a treasure trove of historic sites, with its ancient ruins and medieval castles serving as a testament to the island's rich cultural heritage. The most famous of these sites is the Valley of the Temples, which features some of the best-preserved Greek ruins in the world. From the Temple of Concord to the Temple of Juno, the Valley of the Temples is a must-visit for history buffs.

Another iconic site is the Cattedrale di Monreale, which features a stunning blend of Norman, Byzantine, and Arabic architecture. This cathedral is famous for its intricate mosaics, which depict scenes from the Old and New Testaments.

For those interested in medieval history, the Castello Ursino is a must-visit. Built in the 13th century, this castle has played a pivotal role in Sicilian history, serving as a fortress, a royal residence, and even a prison at various points in time. Today, the castle houses the Museo Civico, which features a fascinating collection of artifacts dating back to the Norman era.

Must- Visit Historic Sites

Valley of the Temples in Agrigento is a vast archaeological park featuring well-preserved ancient Greek temples, including the Temple of Concordia, Temple of Hera, and Temple of Olympian Zeus. It is a UNESCO World Heritage site and one of the most impressive ancient sites in Sicily.

The **Roman Amphitheatre in Catania** dates back to the 2nd century AD and is one of the largest and best-preserved amphitheatres in Italy. It could hold up to 15,000 spectators and was used for gladiatorial games, animal hunts, and public events.

The **Cathedral of Monreale in Palermo** is a stunning example of Norman architecture and features exquisite mosaics and decorative elements. It was built in the 12th century and is considered one of the greatest works of Norman architecture in Sicily.

The **Greek Theatre in Syracuse** is a well-preserved ancient theatre that dates back to the 5th century BC. It could seat up to 15,000 spectators and was used for performances of plays and other cultural events.

Villa Romana del Casale in Piazza Armerina is a Roman villa dating back to the 4th century AD, featuring stunning mosaics that depict scenes from daily life, mythology, and hunting. It is a UNESCO World Heritage site and a unique example of ancient Roman art and architecture.

The Cathedral of Cefalù is a beautiful Norman cathedral located on the northern coast of Sicily. It was built in the 12th century and features stunning Byzantine mosaics, intricate carvings, and a unique fusion of Norman, Arab, and Byzantine architectural styles.

The Temple of Concordia in Agrigento is one of the best-preserved ancient Greek temples in the world. It was built in the 5th century BC and is considered a masterpiece of Doric architecture.

The Baroque Towns of Val di Noto, including Noto, Ragusa, Modica, and Scicli, are a group of charming towns in southeastern Sicily that feature stunning examples of

Baroque architecture. They were rebuilt in the 18th century following a devastating earthquake and are now UNESCO World Heritage sites.

The Norman Palace in Palermo is a magnificent palace complex that was built by the Norman kings in the 12th century. It features stunning mosaics, chapels, and royal apartments, as well as the famous Palatine Chapel with its intricate Byzantine mosaics.

Segesta Archaeological Site is an ancient Greek archaeological site located in western Sicily. It features a well-preserved Doric temple, a theatre, and other ancient ruins, and is surrounded by stunning natural scenery.

CONCLUSION

Final Thoughts

Sicily is an extraordinary place that will leave an indelible impression on anyone who visits. Its rich history, stunning landscapes, and delicious cuisine are just a few of the reasons why it is such a unique and fascinating destination. Whether you're interested in exploring ancient ruins, lounging on pristine beaches, or sampling some of the best food in the world, Sicily has something to offer everyone.

One of the most striking aspects of Sicily is its incredible mix of cultures. From the Greeks and Romans to the Normans and Arabs, the island has been shaped by a long and complex history of conquest and colonization. This diversity is evident in the island's architecture, art, and cuisine, which blend elements from different cultures in fascinating and unexpected ways. Exploring Sicily's many cities and towns is like taking a journey through time, with each one offering its own unique blend of history and culture.

. From the rugged mountains of the interior to the crystal-clear waters of the Mediterranean, Sicily boasts some of the most spectacular scenery in Europe. Hiking in the Nebrodi or Madonie mountains, taking a dip in the turquoise waters of the Aeolian Islands, or wandering through the citrus groves and olive groves of the countryside are just a few of the outdoor activities that await visitors to the island.

Sicilian food is a reflection of the island's complex history, with influences from Italy, Greece, Spain, and North Africa. From the seafood-rich dishes of the coast to the hearty meat dishes of the interior, Sicilian cuisine is a feast for the senses. And let's not forget the island's famous sweet treats, like cannoli, cassata, and granita.

Overall, Sicily is a destination that offers something for everyone. Whether you're interested in history, culture, nature, or food, this incredible island has it all. And with so much to see and do, you'll never run out of things to explore.

Where to Go Next

As you prepare to leave Sicily, you may find yourself feeling a sense of sadness at the thought of saying goodbye to this amazing island. However, there are plenty of other exciting destinations to explore throughout Italy and beyond.

If you're looking to continue your Italian adventure after exploring Sicily, there are plenty of other destinations to consider. Here are just a few:

> Tuscany - Known for its beautiful countryside, world-class art and architecture, and delicious food and wine, Tuscany is a must-visit destination for anyone traveling to Italy. Highlights include Florence, Siena, and the rolling hills of the Chianti region.

- Rome - The eternal city needs no introduction. Home to some of the world's most famous landmarks, including the Colosseum, the Pantheon, and the Vatican, Rome is a must-see destination for anyone interested in history, art, or architecture.

- Venice - Known as the "City of Canals," Venice is one of the most romantic and unique cities in the world. From its beautiful bridges and canals to its incredible art and architecture, Venice is a destination that is sure to captivate visitors.

- Amalfi Coast - Located on the southern coast of Italy, the Amalfi Coast is famous for its picturesque towns, dramatic cliffs, and turquoise waters. Whether you're looking to soak up the sun on a beach or explore charming villages like Positano and Ravello, the Amalfi Coast is a destination that is sure to delight.

- Milan - Known for its fashion, design, and art scene, Milan is a bustling and cosmopolitan city that is a must-visit for anyone interested in contemporary culture. Highlights include the iconic Duomo cathedral, the Leonardo da Vinci

Printed in Great Britain
by Amazon

21909274R00066